Double Stop Shifting

for the cello

Book One

by Cassia Harvey

CHP219

©2013 by C. Harvey Publications All Rights Reserved.

www.charveypublications.com - print books
www.learnstrings.com - PDF downloadable books
www.harveystringarrangements.com - chamber music

Double Stop Shifting for the Cello, Book One

Cassia Harvey

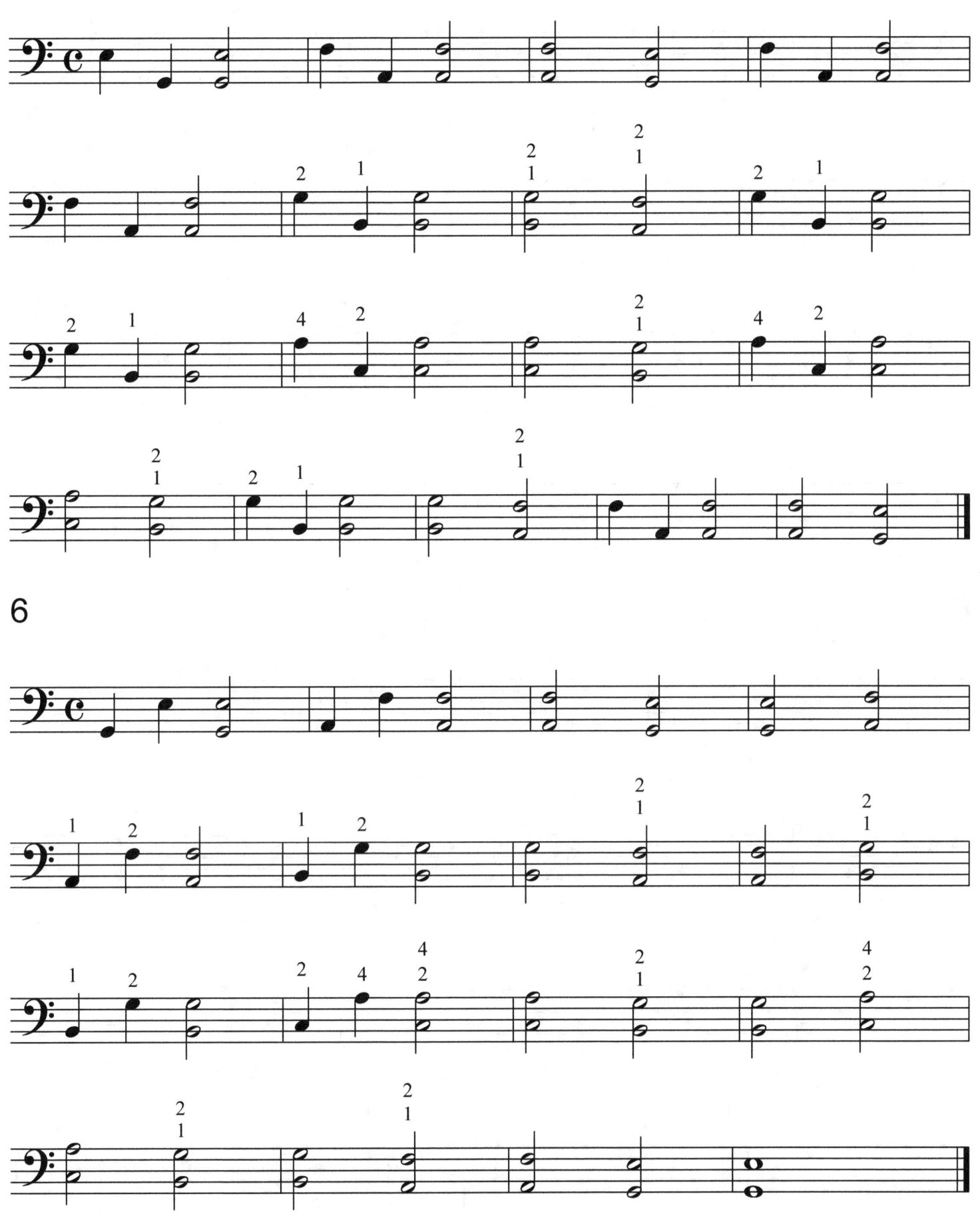

Double Stop Shifting for the Cello, Book One

33

Double Stop Shifting for the Cello, Book One

34

35

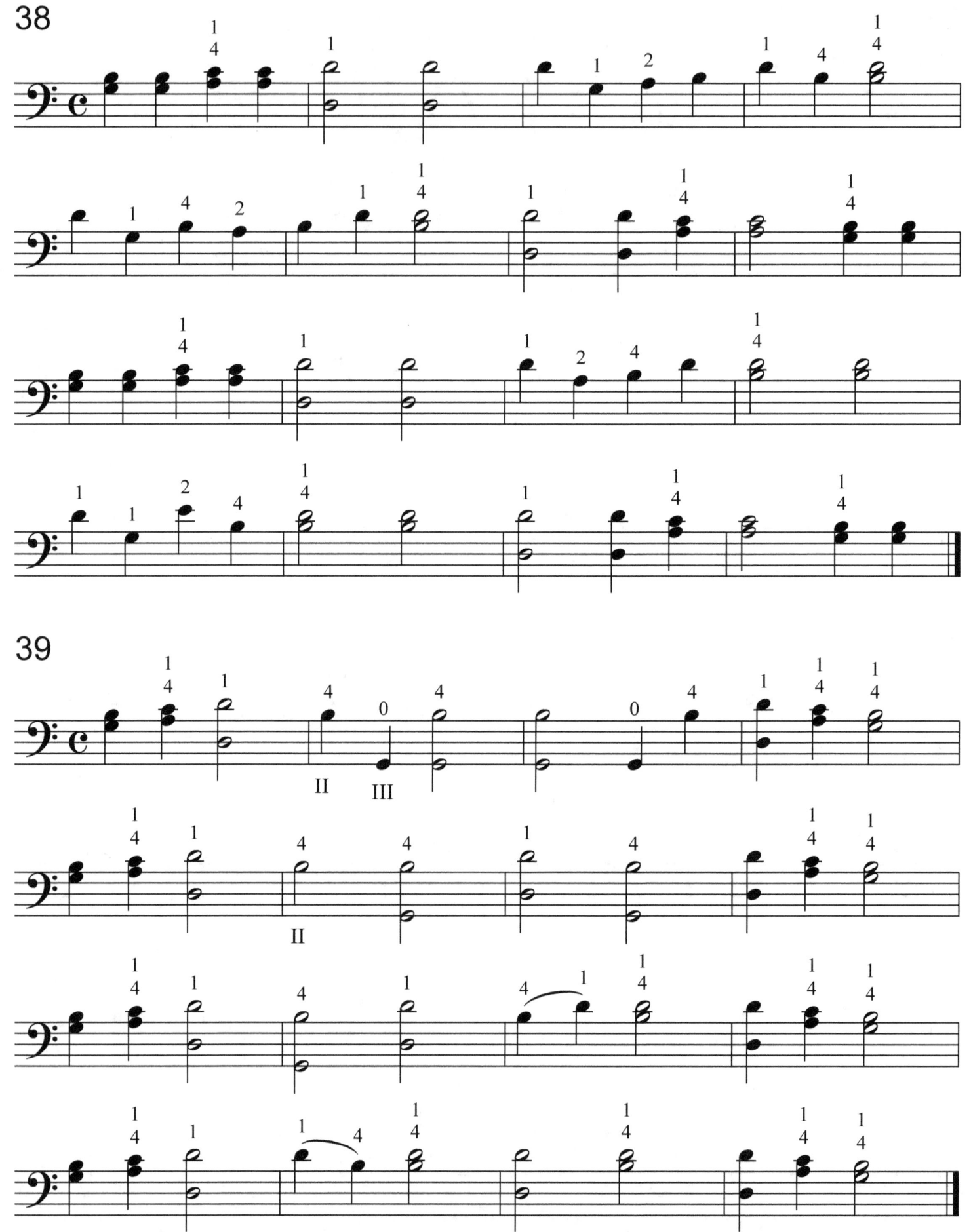

Double Stop Shifting for the Cello, Book One 21

Double Stop Shifting for the Cello, Book One

Double Stop Shifting for the Cello, Book One

25

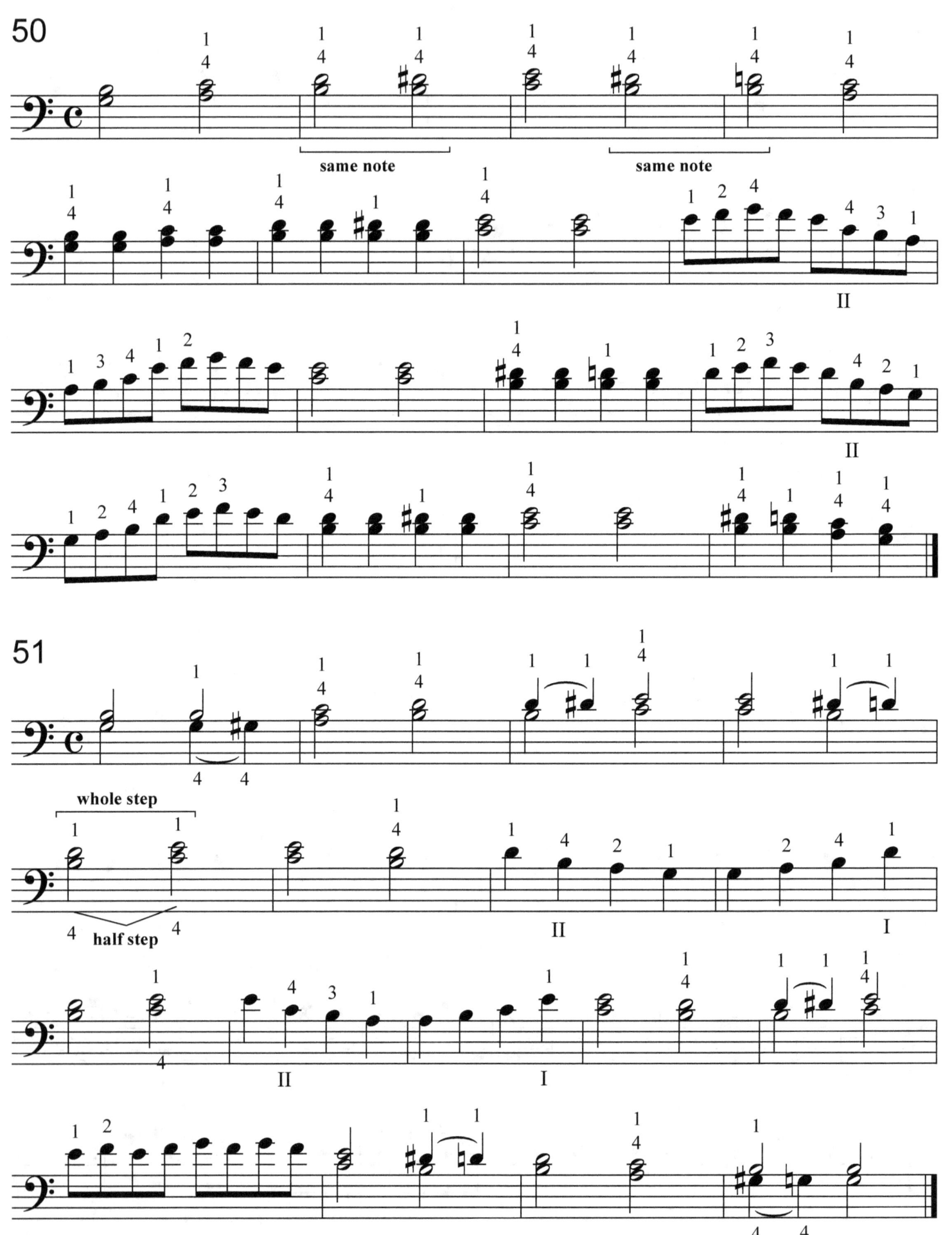

Double Stop Shifting for the Cello, Book One

Double Stop Shifting for the Cello, Book One

Double Stop Shifting for the Cello, Book One
31

60

Also available from www.charveypublications.com: CHP348
The Romberg Sonata in C Major Study Book for Cello

Note: The Sonata is broken up into sections in this study book. The complete piece is at the back of the book.

Sonata, First Movement
Section One: Measures 1-16

Sonata Op. 43 No. 2, by Bernhard Romberg
edited by F. Jansen, C. Harvey
Exercises by Cassia Harvey

Learning the Notes/Intonation
Measures 1-3